Sex Education in
Schools

Essential Viewpoints

SEX EDUCATION IN
SCHOOLS
BY KEKLA MAGOON

Content Consultant
Michael McGee, M.Ed.
Educator, Trainer, Facilitator, Coach

ABDO
Publishing Company

CREDITS

Published by ABDO Publishing Company, 8000 West 78th Street, Edina, Minnesota 55439. Copyright © 2010 by Abdo Consulting Group, Inc. International copyrights reserved in all countries. No part of this book may be reproduced in any form without written permission from the publisher. The Essential Library™ is a trademark and logo of ABDO Publishing Company.

Printed in the United States.

Editor: Amy Van Zee
Copy Editor: Paula Lewis
Interior Design and Production: Nicole Brecke
Cover Design: Nicole Brecke

Library of Congress Cataloging-in-Publication Data
Magoon, Kekla.
  Sex education in schools / by Kekla Magoon.
      p. cm. — (Essential viewpoints)
  Includes bibliographical references and index.
  ISBN 978-1-60453-536-5
  1. Sex instruction—United States. I. Title.
  HQ57.5.A3M24 2009
  613.9071—dc22

                                        2008034917

TABLE OF CONTENTS

Sex education addresses one of the biggest decisions a person will ever make: when to have sex.

SAFER SEX
VERSUS ABSTINENCE

The question of whether or not to have sex is one of the most important considerations most people experience. For some, the decision is very easy. For other people, the decision is much more complicated and can be stressful.

Many things influence the decision to have sex. Love, romance, physical attraction, and intimacy are all very appealing aspects of sexuality. However, there are significant, life-altering consequences that can come with sex, such as having children and entering a committed relationship or marriage. Health issues must also be considered. These include the possibility of exposing oneself to sexually transmitted infections.

For most people, these factors make the decision whether or not to have sex more difficult. What is the best way to learn about the different sexual choices a person can make? Is there one solution that could work for everyone? These questions are particularly significant for young people. Many individuals and groups work to answer these questions. All these groups have young people's best interest at heart, but they have very different ideas about what is most helpful for teaching young people about sex.

"Sexuality education ideally would encompass sexual knowledge, beliefs, attitudes, values, and behaviors. Included would be anatomy, physiology, and biochemistry of the sexual response system, gender roles, identity and personality, and thoughts, feelings, behaviors, and relationships. In addition, moral and ethical concerns, group and cultural diversity, and social change would be addressed. Unfortunately, sexuality education classes in the United States fall far from this ideal."[1]
— *Wendy Stock, author of* Sex Education

What Is Sex Education?

Sex education is the process of gaining knowledge about sexuality, sex, and intimate relationships. It also involves forming opinions and beliefs about what sexual feelings and behaviors are right and appropriate. For most people, sex education has many different components. Sexual knowledge comes from many different sources, some formal and some informal. Sources of sexual information often include parents, teachers, friends, and media.

When formal sex education takes place at home or in schools, it is usually intended to provide students with a core set of facts about sexuality. Not everyone agrees on what information is best to include in formal sex education. Several different approaches can be taken. These include abstinence, birth control, and safer sex.

Terminology: Abstinence

Words and phrases people use in talking about abstinence include: purity, virginity, chastity, innocence, modesty, waiting until marriage, and saving oneself for marriage.

What Is Abstinence?

Abstinence means voluntarily choosing not to have sex. Many people choose to practice abstinence by waiting until they are married to have sex. People choose abstinence for many reasons. Some feel that sex before marriage is morally wrong. Others abstain because their religious tradition requires them to wait. Some want to avoid the emotional attachment that comes with the intimacy of sex. Others seek to protect themselves against sexually transmitted infections and unwanted pregnancy by avoiding sexual contact.

People who practice abstinence may think about sex and even talk about sex, but they have made the decision not to have intercourse until they are married.

What about Birth Control and Safer Sex?

Birth control refers to the precautions sexually active people take to prevent pregnancy. Forms of birth control that women use include birth control pills, diaphragms, and intrauterine devices. Men can use condoms or spermicide. Birth control is also called contraception.

Using birth control during sex is often referred to as having "safer sex." While birth control helps prevent unplanned pregnancies, some forms of birth control also

Terminology: Birth Control

Words and phrases people use in talking about birth control include: birth planning, contraception, preventing conception, family planning, fertility control, and safer sex.

help prevent sexually transmitted infections from spreading. People who use birth control methods often do so with both of these things in mind.

THE SEX EDUCATION DEBATE

Some people believe that everyone should be encouraged to practice abstinence before marriage. They believe that waiting to have sex is a good moral decision. They believe that if a society talks a lot about abstinence, more people will choose to practice it. Many pro-abstinence citizens hope that all communities, schools, and families will teach young people that abstinence until marriage is the best way to approach sexual behavior. Some religious groups feel a moral obligation to educate people about abstinence, as well.

Others believe that each person makes his or her sexual decisions based upon many different factors. They believe that it is unrealistic to believe that every person will choose to practice abstinence. They believe young people should be educated about birth control and safer sex so that, when and if they decide to have intercourse, they will know how to protect themselves.

These Seattle students discuss their opinions about sex education.

Touchy Subject

Debating sex education, birth control, and abstinence can be difficult because the subject of the conversation is sex. It can feel awkward to discuss such powerful, personal, and intimate issues in public. Some people believe that sex should not be discussed in public at all. They believe it should be a topic reserved for home and family.

Others believe that keeping sexual conversations behind closed doors leads people to think that sex is something to be ashamed of. They believe that it is important to discuss these issues publicly so that people will not be afraid to ask questions about birth control, abstinence, and sexual health.

BIRTH CONTROL VERSUS ABSTINENCE IN SCHOOLS

The sex education debate focuses on what schools should be allowed to teach young people. Pro-abstinence groups favor schools teaching abstinence only. This does not include discussions of any other forms of birth control or sexual behavior. Some worry that too much talk of sex will not reinforce the belief that premarital sex should be avoided.

Birth control groups support the teaching of abstinence, but they prefer to see it taught as part of a broader conversation on birth control and sexual health. They believe that it is better for people to understand their options in order to protect themselves when they do have sex. These groups would like to see all youth educated on birth control and safer sex.

Schools across the nation struggle in deciding what material to teach in their health classes. Educators feel an obligation to give students all the available health information, including lessons on sexual health, sexually transmitted infections, and birth control. However, they also feel an obligation to provide positive moral guidance for students by encouraging them to abstain from sexual behavior until they are ready, whether or not that means waiting until marriage.

There is no easy answer for schools. Federal law does not specifically limit what portions of sexual education can and cannot be taught in schools. It also does not require schools to teach about every aspect of sexuality. Pro-abstinence groups want the government to support them by creating laws that prevent schools

Decision Theory

How do individuals make choices? Decision theory explains the factors that go into each decision a person makes. These decisions may happen in a split second (such as a pedestrian crossing the street against the light) or over a matter of minutes, days, or years (such as a person deciding whether or not to have sex).

When faced with several options, a person considers the benefits and risks of each choice. Then, they compare the benefits of each choice with those of the other choices. Eventually, a person determines that one choice has more benefit and less risk. Or, a person may decide that one choice is worth a substantial risk because of its substantial benefit.

For example, the pedestrian may be late for school. Is it worth hurrying across the street in front of an oncoming truck to get to class on time? The benefit of hurrying is punctuality. The risk is getting hit by the truck. The benefit of waiting is safety. The risk is getting in trouble for being late.

Weighing the benefits and risks of sexual activity is usually a longer, more complicated process. The sex education debate is very much about decision theory. What information will enable young people to view "risk" and "benefit" in ways that will lead them to make good sexual decisions?

from teaching about birth control. Pro-birth control groups favor laws that uphold their right to teach all points of view to students.

One thing the law does require is the separation of church and state. Because many people view abstinence-only teaching as a religious conviction, this is important to the sex education debate. Not everyone who chooses abstinence does so for religious reasons. However, many people who advocate abstinence do so on the basis of their religion. It can be difficult to distinguish what is morally right for everyone from the values of a particular religion.

MAKING THE DECISION

Although people's sexual choices are made in private, many people want to have public conversations that will help others make good sexual decisions. Birth control advocates and abstinence advocates feel very strongly about their positions. Is there a middle ground to be reached? How should communities, the law, and schools respond to the call for sex education? —

This Kansas student discusses sex education at a Senate meeting.

In 1946, the American Social Hygiene Association held a fund-raiser featuring boxer Joe Louis, right, "knocking out" venereal disease.

SEX EDUCATION
IN U.S. HISTORY

In one sense, sex education is ageless. But the debate over sex education today is a relatively modern concept. Within the twentieth and twenty-first centuries, the nation's views about sex and sex education have changed greatly.

Sexual Revolution in the Early 1900s

In the late nineteenth century, sex was not only a socially taboo subject, but with legislation such as the Comstock Act of 1873, distribution of "immoral" or "lewd" material was banned. This included birth control information. In the early twentieth century, people thought about sex education, but talking about it was socially awkward. Women were fighting for the right to vote, and a major part of the motivation was women's desire to be in control of their destinies. A related movement toward sex education emerged. To many women, sex education represented the ability to control one's body and one's sexual decisions.

In 1913, Grace Dodge helped establish the American Social Hygiene Association. The group was officially launched in 1915. This became the first organization to promote sex education. The organization was concerned with prostitution, sexually transmitted

Turn of the Century Changes

Many things changed in U.S. society at the beginning of the twentieth century, and many of the changes affected young people. Cities were growing and new kinds of jobs became available. Education became important to more people, so young people stayed in school longer. Coeducational high schools and colleges allowed teenagers to spend time together away from their parents. Teens began going out with friends and dating alone, instead of courting with their families watching. It slowly became more socially acceptable for unmarried people of opposite sexes to touch each other in public, such as holding hands and kissing.

infections (venereal diseases), and other health risks. They focused especially on vulnerable communities. "Social hygienists" also believed in women's rights and called public attention to the different standards held for men and women in sexual life.

The First "Teenagers"

In 1904, psychologist G. Stanley Hall first coined the term *adolescents*. Before then, adolescents were not considered their own social group. Once children passed through puberty, they were considered old enough to begin preparing for marriage and work.

However, in the first part of the twentieth century, people were marrying later in life than those in earlier generations. This delay created a new social group of Americans that, in some sense, had never existed before: teenagers.

As people waited until they were older to get married, society changed. For the first time in history, there were significant numbers of young, unmarried people. Sex before marriage became more common. It was still frowned upon, but it occurred. This increased the need for sex education. More people and organizations began teaching about sexual health, usually by discouraging premarital sex.

Most sex education was directed at preparation for marriage and a healthy family life.

REDEVELOPING FAMILY VALUES

The social upheaval of the early twentieth century calmed down during the 1930s. The Great Depression had citizens concerned with food, shelter, and basic necessities. When the United States entered World War II in 1941, the nation banded together to support the war effort. Many men became soldiers, and women took jobs in

Marriage Culture

In 1950, the U.S. Census Bureau reported that the marriage rate was 68 percent for all people over age 15. There were few divorces at that time: only 2 percent of adults were divorced. By 1980, the marriage rate declined to 63 percent. The divorce rate increased: 5 percent of adults were divorced in 1980. By 2006, the marriage rate was 51 percent and 12 percent of adults were divorced or separated. Today, people in the United States are generally marrying later in life than they were in the mid-twentieth century. The higher divorce rate today means many children are affected by parents who are divorced. The divorce rate has made some people skeptical of marriage in general. It leads others to believe (or worry) that they may not ever get married. This perception presents a challenge for sex educators, especially those who want youth to wait until marriage to have sex.

The principle of abstinence education is "no sex until marriage." Abstinence educators often try to counter teens' skepticism by teaching about the benefits of healthy marriage. Comprehensive health educators, on the other hand, may also refer to the divorce rate. They might use it as an example of why "committed monogamous relationship" is a more accurate term today than "marriage."

factories and offices. Some of those jobs had never been open to women before. This began to change the way men and women viewed each other's roles in society.

The war ended in 1945, and the years that followed were a relatively calm and quiet time in the United States. Soldiers returning from the war married and began raising families. Many women left the workforce and returned to being housewives and full-time mothers. Marriage and family became very important. The nation took pride in its ability to form a solid moral foundation—citizens believed strongly in capitalism and "the American way of life." Through the 1950s, the U.S. government encouraged its citizens to live within this moral code. They worried about the effects communism and other lifestyles could have on the nation.

"When men and women fail to form stable marriages, the first result is a vast expansion of government attempts to cope with the terrible social needs that result. There is scarcely a dollar that state and federal government spends on social programs that is not driven in large part by family fragmentation: crime, poverty, drug abuse, teen pregnancy, school failure, mental and physical health problems."[1]
—*Maggie Gallagher, author of* The Stakes: Why We Need Marriage

SEXUAL REVOLUTION IN THE 1960s AND 1970s

A second sexual revolution occurred in the 1960s and 1970s. These were two decades of major turmoil in the United States. Many people had lost faith in the ability of the federal government to look out for its citizens. Many issues were at stake. African Americans struggled for civil rights and an end to segregation. Women fought for equal work opportunities and equal treatment in society. They no longer wanted to be treated differently than men in their work, family, relationships, and sexuality. These decades also marked key Supreme Court decisions related to women's reproductive health. In 1965, the U.S. Supreme Court ruled that laws prohibiting birth control were unconstitutional. In 1973, the U.S. Supreme Court ruled in *Roe v. Wade* that abortion was legal.

The United States was also involved in the Vietnam War. The U.S. public was divided in its opinions about U.S. involvement. Some supported the war and others protested it. Young people were among the strongest opponents of the war. College students and teens participated in mass demonstrations for peace. When the war did not end quickly, many became angry and disillusioned with

The hippie "free love" movement challenged traditional ideas about sex.

the government. Many young people rebelled against "traditional" ways of life. Marriage, monogamy, responsibility, education, regular employment, and settled family life were criticized. Young people proclaimed free love and independence. They also set out to change the way people lived. Sex was treated casually and many experimented with drugs and alcohol. These youth were called "hippies" or "flower children." Many wandered the nation in search of what they thought would be a better way of life than what their parents had known.

CHANGING SEX EDUCATION

Not all young people lived as hippies, but their ideas influenced an entire generation. Sex educators had to respond. Since more young people had decided to begin having sex outside of marriage, sex educators began talking about reducing risk. They began teaching about seeking committed relationships, using contraception, and avoiding sexually transmitted infections (STIs). The U.S. Food and Drug Administration approved the sale of oral contraceptive pills in 1960, making birth control much more available. This was a major change from the time when sex educators used their knowledge to help prepare youth for entering marriage. It was also a controversial time in the

Cold War: Culture of Fear

The cold war (mid-1940s to early 1990s) between the United States and the Union of Soviet Socialist Republics (USSR) was a war of ideas. It represented a conflict between two opposing styles of government: capitalism and communism. Tension was high in the United States during that time. Americans became fearful of things that were different. They worried that change could hurt them.

During the uncertain times, people relied on marriage and family for stability and protection. For too many people, though, the perfect family lifestyle of the 1950s was a false front. Some people did not want to be married or live the way they were expected to at the time. Even some people who were happily married and believed in family values felt stifled. The situation was ripe for another social upheaval— a sexual revolution.

nation's history. Many of the values people had long considered "traditional" and "American" were being challenged.

The Era of HIV/AIDS

The hippies' "free-love" movement died down by the 1980s. The mood of the nation slowly turned more conservative. Numerous social and political groups promoted a return to traditional values.

In 1981, doctors began to take notice that many people were acquiring a strange disease. In the following years, doctors called the disease acquired immunodeficiency syndrome (AIDS). AIDS was soon linked to the human immunodeficiency virus (HIV), a sexually transmitted virus. Over the next ten years, any remaining talk of free love steadily turned into talk of safer sex and abstinence. Prior to AIDS and HIV, the biggest perceived risk involved in sex was pregnancy. People had worried about STIs, but none were widely considered life threatening. When HIV/AIDS appeared, though, people became afraid. Sex suddenly seemed quite risky. Unprotected sex with an infected partner could end a life.

HIV/AIDS radically changed the way Americans viewed sex and sexuality. It also changed sex education. A great divide developed between sex educators in the 1980s and 1990s. Some wanted to follow the sex educators of the 1960s and continue to teach about safer sex and risk reduction. Others wanted to return to the earlier model of discouraging premarital sex and preparing young men and women for monogamous marriage. The debate today is still based on these extremes.

THE SEX EDUCATION DEBATE TODAY

Public schools throughout the United States have been offering sex education programs since the 1960s. The programs differ in various school districts.

In the debate, some people push for abstinence-only sex education. They want little discussion in schools

The First Lady of Contraception

Margaret Sanger, a maternity nurse and birth control advocate of the early 1900s, was often referred to as the First Lady of Contraception. Sanger believed strongly that women should have the right to control their own bodies and choose whether or not to begin parenthood. In 1916, she opened the first U.S. birth control clinic in Brooklyn, New York, where she helped women and men learn about family planning.

about sexual behavior. They want educators to teach students that it is right and good to wait until marriage to have sex. They want educators to avoid talking to students about sexual intercourse, birth control, and safer sex practices.

Others in the debate push for comprehensive sex education. They want students to learn more about sexual behavior. They want educators to teach students about abstinence, but also to explain sexual intercourse, birth control, and safer sex practices. They believe this is a better approach.

Still others think the goal of sex education is to help young people to grow into sexually healthy adults. They want students to learn about decision making, assertiveness skills, effective communication, and how to develop good relationships. This group sometimes includes both the pro-birth control advocates and the abstinence-only advocates. ⌐

*Musician Freddie Mercury died in 1991 of AIDS. His death raised
public awareness about the serious threat of the disease.*

A Washington school nurse teaches about birth control, sexually transmitted diseases, and abstinence in a health education course.

SEX EDUCATION TOPICS

While people debated whether sex education belongs at home or in schools, some state governments decided to take on sex education as part of their responsibility to students. This decision has not quieted the debate.

As of 2008, the District of Columbia and 18 states require sex education as part of school curricula. The other 32 states do not require it. Some states request parental permission before students can participate in sex education classes. Other states assign all students to sex education classes, but allow parents to remove their children from the class if they are opposed to the topics that will be taught.

COMPONENTS OF SEX EDUCATION

Public schools provide health classes for middle school and high school students. These classes usually include a component of sex education. In some school systems, sex education may be a class of its own. There is no standard national sex education curriculum that must be followed in the United States. Thus, sex education programs may be structured differently in different school systems. However, sex education courses throughout the country tend to contain some of the same lessons and information.

Sex education usually has many components. Students learn about their reproductive anatomy. This includes a discussion of changes that occur in the body during puberty, as well as how pregnancy occurs physiologically. Teachers explain the physical act of sex, talk about the consequences of sexual activity, and discuss safer sex practices. Some school districts choose to present all of these components. Others may spend more time on some topics, but very little or no time on others.

REPRODUCTIVE SCIENCE

Health classes and sex education classes usually introduce students to human anatomy, including the reproductive organs. Students may be shown pictures of the outside and inside of female and male bodies. They usually learn the names and functions of each part of the male and female reproductive systems. This information is taught because educators believe it is important for young people to know and understand how their physical bodies are built and how they work.

Students then may be taught how those parts interact during sex. Some schools teach only about

Peer Pressure

Numerous sex education programs place some emphasis on avoiding peer pressure. The idea of controlling one's own body and sexual decisions is an important lesson in sex education. Abstinence educators urge youth to resist any peer pressure to have premarital sex. Comprehensive sex educators urge youth to be sure that, no matter when they choose to have sex, it is a mutual decision and not the result of pressure.

vaginal intercourse between a man and a woman. Other schools also talk about same-sex partners, masturbation, oral sex, and anal intercourse.

PREGNANCY AND CHILDBIRTH

Sex education classes teach students that sex can lead to pregnancy. They teach that having a baby is a wonderful event when a couple is ready to be parents. They teach that it can also be a challenge if it happens at an unexpected or unplanned time in a couple's life.

Schools often have two things in mind when they teach about pregnancy. First, schools educate about what the experience of childbirth may be like. Second, the school usually warns young couples about the major burdens of having a child when not physically, emotionally, or financially prepared.

Talking about pregnancy and childbirth may involve looking at pictures of pregnant women and babies and learning the stages of fetal development. In some schools, this may also include watching a video of a baby being born. Some students are assigned a project in which they must carry around a doll, a bag of flour, a goldfish in a bowl, or an egg for a period of time. These assignments help

This student participated in a program designed to teach girls about sex and relationships by wearing an "empathy belly."

students begin to understand the amount of time and responsibility it takes to be a good parent.

Sexually Transmitted Infections

Most sex education programs teach students about sexually transmitted infections (STIs). STIs are passed between people who have sexual contact with each other. The two basic causes of STIs are viruses and bacteria. Viruses are highly infectious and may have some possible treatments, but they cannot be cured. The human immunodeficiency virus (HIV) is an example of a sexually transmitted virus. STIs caused by bacteria may be treatable, or even curable, through antibiotics. Gonorrhea is an example of sexually transmitted bacteria.

Learning about STIs may involve discussing different infections, how they affect the body, and how they are spread. Students may be shown drawings or even photographs of STIs on real people's genitalia. Teachers usually go over the signs and symptoms of several common STIs, their long-term effects, and treatment options.

Sex education programs that teach about STIs are intended to inform young people about the risks that can be present when people have sex. Educators hope that talking about these illnesses will discourage young people from having unprotected sex or from having sex at all. They also know it is important for youth to be able to recognize the signs and symptoms of an STI and seek treatment if they experience one.

Common STIs

Human papillomavirus (HPV) is the most common STI. There are more than 100 different versions of the virus. Symptoms include genital warts. Some people infected with HPV never show symptoms.

Herpes is caused by a virus and usually appears as genital warts. It can also be present in the mouth as cold sores. Once a person has herpes, they have it for life, even if the symptoms fade.

Bacteria cause gonorrhea. Antibiotics can cure gonorrhea once it is diagnosed.

Syphilis bacteria cause sores to appear on and around the genitals. Syphilis is spread through contact with the sores on another person. In early stages, syphilis can be cured with antibiotics.

Human Immunodeficiency Virus

The human immunodeficiency virus (HIV) is the sexually transmitted virus that causes acquired immunodeficiency syndrome (AIDS). The HIV virus is transmitted only through blood or body fluid contact. It is most concentrated in blood, semen, vaginal secretions, and breast milk.

The human body can carry HIV for many years without showing signs. Health professionals recommend that people who have exchanged blood or body fluids with others, such as through sexual activity, should be tested for HIV.

Globally, HIV/AIDS is considered a pandemic. Nearly 40 million people worldwide were living with HIV as of 2006. In 2006, an estimated 2.9 million people died from AIDS.

ABSTINENCE

Sex education programs include abstinence as an option. To abstain from something means not to do it. Students who practice abstinence are choosing not to have sex. Most schools talk about abstinence as the best and safest way for students to protect themselves against pregnancy, STIs, and other life-altering consequences. Some schools also talk about abstinence as a good moral choice, and they discourage anyone from having sex before marriage. Many people believe that talking about abstinence is the only appropriate way to handle conversations about sex in school.

HEALTHY RELATIONSHIPS

Sex education curricula usually include discussions on building healthy relationships. Students learn about emotional connections and the time and energy involved in maintaining a romantic relationship. They may discuss examples of unhealthy relationships, abuse scenarios, and how relationships are affected by each person's own self-esteem.

Some schools talk about various ways that young couples can be emotionally close and physically intimate without actually having sexual intercourse. Alternative suggestions often include holding hands, hugging or cuddling, kissing, or exchanging back or foot massages.

Birth Control and Safer Sex Methods

A condom is a protective sheath placed on the penis prior to intercourse. Condoms may be made of latex, polyurethane, or animal skin. They are highly effective, though not foolproof, in preventing pregnancy and STI transmission.

Hormonal contraceptives must be prescribed by a physician. These contraceptives regulate hormones that control ovulation. Birth control pills must be taken daily. Birth control medication is also available in patches applied to the skin, a cervical ring, or regular hormone injections. Hormonal contraceptives do not protect against STI transmission.

An oral dam is a square of latex that can be used as a barrier during oral sex with a woman. Used properly, these may be effective in preventing STI transmission.

A diaphragm is a rubber or soft plastic disc women use as a barrier to block sperm during intercourse. Diaphragms do not protect against STI transmission.

Spermicide is designed to kill sperm before it can reach and fertilize an egg. Spermicide does not protect against STI transmission.

The intrauterine device (IUD) is for use by women and must be inserted by a physician. It is a small Y-shaped device that prevents the sperm from fertilizing the egg and changes the lining of the uterus to prevent pregnancy. It does not prevent STI transmission.

Safer Sex

Some sex education classes discuss methods of safer sex, in addition to supporting abstinence. Safer sex practices include using contraceptives and barriers to STI transmission. Condoms and birth control pills are two commonly discussed items. Students may be given information on how to obtain and use these and other protection methods. They are usually taught about the kind of protection each item provides, especially whether or not it protects against both pregnancy and STI transmission.

Many schools choose to use the term *safer sex* instead of *safe sex* because they want students to understand that there is always some risk involved in sexual activity. Schools that teach safer sex believe it is important for young people to understand how to protect themselves if they choose to have sex.

Abstinence Pledges

Some schools, many religious programs, and some families go beyond simply teaching abstinence. They encourage young people to take a vow or make a pledge to practice abstinence. These may include a Promise of Abstinence, a Vow of Chastity, a Purity Pledge, or a Commitment to Wait.

Some youth choose to wear rings or other jewelry to symbolize their purity, chastity, or abstinence. Jewelry items serve as both a public statement of their choice as well as a personal reminder of their commitment to abstinence.

Some schools use a doll called "Baby Think It Over" in sex education classes. The doll simulates a real infant to give hands-on experience.

Some state legislatures have held hearings to discuss the issue of regulating sex education curriculum in public schools.

GOVERNMENT RESPONSIBILITY

hy is it so difficult to decide what kind of sex education students in the United States receive? School districts around the country vary their sex education curriculum based on differing local, state, and federal standards. How are those choices made? And who should be in charge of making the decisions?

The debate over sex education has been going on in schools for decades. Groups on both sides of the issue have tried to push the debate toward their point of view. They may work locally, statewide, or nationally to try to get sex education curricula to conform to what they want.

A Legal Debate?

Today, the sex education debate is almost solely a discussion of what is moral and what is practical. Opinions vary greatly. There is no law prohibiting sex before marriage. There are also no federal laws that require or prohibit sex education for youth. People within the debate disagree about whether there should be such laws.

Should the sex education debate be a matter of federal law? Some people say that federal law should prohibit comprehensive sex education and require abstinence-only sex education. Other people say that federal law should require comprehensive sex education and prohibit abstinence-only sex education. Some people believe sex education should not be written into federal law at all. They may say the decision should be left to the states. Or they may say that federal laws about sex education would violate the right to free speech.

State and Local Regulations

The federal government has not established specific guidelines for sexual health education that apply to all schools in the country. Those laws are left up to the individual state governments to develop. Guidelines for sex education vary widely from state to state. Some states specifically require sex education for all students in certain grades. Some specifically prohibit it for students in lower grades, but allow it for older students. Many states have regulations about the content of sex education curriculum. For instance, states can specify whether classes must promote abstinence first, whether they must teach about HIV/AIDS and other STIs, and if they are permitted to speak about contraception.

Local school districts are responsible for most of the decisions about sex education programs. They rely on state guidelines to help develop their programs, but state guidelines usually leave room for details to be worked out locally. School boards and communities work to develop programs that are accurate and reflect the values of the community.

FEDERAL FUNDING FOR ABSTINENCE-ONLY EDUCATION

The first federal law funding abstinence education was passed in 1981 under the Adolescent Family Life Act. This act provided support for programs that encouraged chastity for pregnancy prevention in young teens. In 1996, President

A Federal Definition

As reported by NARAL Pro-Choice America, the federal definition of an abstinence-only program is one that:

- *has as its exclusive purpose, teaching the social, psychological, and health gains to be realized by abstaining from sexual activity;*
- *teaches abstinence from sexual activity outside marriage as the expected standard for all school age children;*
- *teaches that abstinence from sexual activity is the only certain way to avoid out-of-wedlock pregnancy, sexually transmitted diseases, and other associated health problems;*
- *teaches that a mutually faithful monogamous relationship in the context of marriage is the expected standard of human sexual activity;*
- *teaches that sexual activity outside of the context of marriage is likely to have harmful psychological and physical effects;*
- *teaches that bearing children out-of-wedlock is likely to have harmful consequences for the child, the child's parents, and society.*[2]

The program may not contradict any part of this definition.

Bill Clinton signed legislation to create a $250 million fund that would support five years of abstinence-only education programs. The money would be granted to individual states, which would have to match the federal dollars with state money. Thus, a total of up to $500 million would be spent on abstinence education over five years. In the first year of the funding, 49 states accepted and matched the federal money.

In 2000, a third funding program was created: the Community-Based Abstinence Education Program. The abstinence-only education legislation endorsed by Clinton expired in 2002, but it was reassigned to the Family and Youth Services Bureau. It continues to be funded in much the same way. In 2008, only 33 states accepted the federal money. The other states refused it, believing that abstinence-only education was not working for their students.

Separation of Church and State

Federal funding programs for abstinence education have reenergized an ongoing debate about the separation of church and state. One of the basic principles the United States was founded on is the belief that government and religion should be kept

Catholic popes, such as John Paul II, have publicly condemned birth control methods.

separate. The first ten amendments to the U.S. Constitution are known as the Bill of Rights. The First Amendment prohibits the government from establishing a national religion.

Some people argue that abstinence-only sex education is based on religious values. Therefore, they believe the government should not impose the values of any religion on all its citizens. They claim that, because schools are government entities, teachers should be free to choose to educate students using a broader sex education curriculum.

Comprehensive sex educators do not want state laws that promote abstinence-only education. Religious communities stand at the forefront of the debate, promoting abstinence, and citing their faith as motivation. Comprehensive sex educators argue that if abstinence-only teaching has a religious basis, how can schools legally be bound to present only that side? Legislators must say that abstinence is a moral issue that is not restricted to religion in order to allow such laws to exist.

States Refusing Federal Funds

Arizona, California, Colorado, Connecticut, Iowa, Maine, Massachusetts, Minnesota, Montana, New Jersey, New Mexico, New York, Ohio, Rhode Island, Virginia, and Wisconsin have all refused to receive federal funding for abstinence-only education. California is the only state that declined abstinence-only education funding from the beginning.

In addition, the First Amendment prohibits the government from making laws that prevent free speech. Some people argue that preventing comprehensive sex education in schools violates the right to free speech. In some school districts, for example, sex education teachers are prevented from talking about birth control or distributing condoms. Is it legal for the law to restrict speech and expression in this way? Abstinence educators say yes. Comprehensive sex educators say no.

Who Should Control It?

Related to the legal debate is the basic question of who should be responsible for teaching about sex. There are many sources of information and misinformation that young people encounter as they learn about their own sexuality. So, whom should they turn to? Should it be their parents and families? Should it be schoolteachers? Should it be religious leaders and communities? Should it be pop culture, media, and their peers?

People on both sides of the debate usually agree that it is important for adults to deliberately educate youth about sex, rather than allowing pop culture to influence them. But which adults should be the educators? People on both sides of the debate believe it is vital for parents to discuss sex with their children. They believe this promotes healthy conversations and openness, which will lead young people to make better sexual decisions. Some people feel that parents and families are the only adults who should provide sex education to their own children. They do not think it is helpful for schools and teachers to offer sex education. They believe sex topics should remain private. Some parents worry that the schools will teach their children something

When Should Sex Education Begin?

One of the biggest issues in the sex education debate is determining when young people should start learning about sex topics. Children usually start school at age five or six. Sex education often begins in sixth or seventh grade. Some experts say it should begin earlier.

Some school districts employ developmental psychologists to make recommendations for sexual health curricula. These professionals understand what the body and mind are capable of at different ages. They may be able to explain the way children think about their bodies when they are young, when they reach puberty, and as they grow into teenagers. Knowing this helps educators determine what topics are appropriate at different grade levels.

that they as parents do not support. They want to be in control of their children's sex education.

Many other people believe sex education is an appropriate topic for school classrooms. They believe it is important to have open dialogue about sex issues so that students can have the opportunity to ask questions. They believe sex education is important enough to be part of standard curriculum for all students. They worry that if it is left up to individual parents, then some students may not get complete or accurate information. In addition, some parents find it too difficult to bring up sex topics with their children and appreciate it being handled by the schools. Others feel it is easier to answer children's questions and discuss the topic at home after it has been introduced in the formal classroom setting.

Some people believe sex education topics should be taught by parents and not in public places, such as schools.

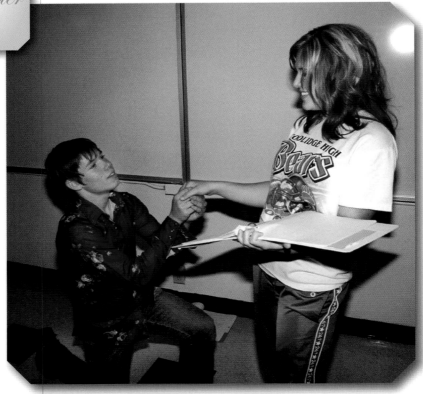

These students engage in a skit that is part of the
"Worth the Wait" program.

ABSTINENCE-ONLY
EDUCATION

bstinence educators and their
supporters strongly believe that
abstinence-only education is the best way to ensure
that young people will make good decisions about
sex. They use many arguments to support their belief

and to bring forth research and statistics to back their claims.

MORALITY

Abstinence education is often based on the moral belief that sex before marriage is wrong. Abstinence educators believe that there is no circumstance under which unmarried teenagers should be having sex. Therefore, they believe it is completely irrelevant to teach youth about how to have safer, protected sex. They believe that promoting that moral code is the only option for teens. By presenting abstinence in a positive light, it will prevent youth from engaging in sexual behavior.

Much of the current movement toward abstinence education has emerged from within religious communities. These groups are often motivated by a moral commitment to reduce premarital sex among young people. Some abstinence educators are not motivated by their religion but agree that premarital sex is morally wrong.

"If premarital sex came in a bottle, it would probably have to carry a Surgeon General's warning, something like the one on a package of cigarettes. There's no way to have premarital sex without hurting someone."[1]
—*Colleen Kelly Mast, author of* Sex Respect

100 Percent Effective, Every Time

Abstinence educators remind students that abstinence is the only 100 percent effective method of birth control. This is one of the central arguments that abstinence education supporters use to make their case. They believe that sexual activity should be described as a serious emotional and physical risk when it occurs before marriage. Abstinence educators see this as a way of protecting young people.

Emphasizes Relationships

Abstinence educators want to see sexual health education focus more on what it takes to build strong character and healthy interpersonal relationships. They believe that young people should be taught to seek strong relationships that are based on commitment and emotional connection before exploring sexual behavior. Then they will learn how to make good relationship decisions and good sexual decisions. The goal is that young people will develop self-restraint and self-respect as a result of abstinence education.

Abstinence education also may focus on resisting peer pressure and the importance of being able

Purity rings are an outward symbol some people wear to show their commitment to abstinence.

to make decisions. Programs are structured to emphasize the value of sexual purity and to make youth see sexual purity as the best goal. They believe that if more young people value abstinence, then two things will happen. First, fewer teens will try to pressure each other into sex. Second, if teens do feel pressure, they will have the self-confidence to say no. Concerns that young people are being pressured into sex before they intend to engage in it is a major part of why abstinence educators want less talk about sexual activity.

Avoiding the Abstract

Abstinence educators consider marriage a concrete concept. They believe students know and understand what marriage means and how to recognize it. Thus, they believe there is no way for a student who commits to abstinence until marriage to have sex too early.

Abstinence educators do not talk about "committed monogamous relationships" between people who are not married. They do not believe it is helpful for youth to learn to wait to have sex until they are "ready." They say that it may be hard for a young person to gauge when he or she is exactly ready. They also believe that it is very easy for teenagers to misjudge their readiness. The only time two people are ready to have sex, they argue, is when they have taken the step of a lifelong commitment to each other in marriage.

Success of Abstinence Pledges

According to research by abstinence educators, young people who pledge abstinence are more likely

"Real abstinence education is essential to reducing out-of-wedlock childbearing, preventing sexually transmitted diseases, and improving emotional and physical well-being among the nation's youth. True abstinence education programs help young people to develop an understanding of commitment, fidelity, and intimacy that will serve them well as the foundations of healthy marital life in the future."[2]
—*Robert Rector,*
Senior Research Fellow,
The Heritage Foundation

to wait until marriage to have sex. The Heritage Foundation reports that 30 percent of youth who take abstinence pledges have sex before marriage, compared to 66 percent of their peers who did not take the pledge. Abstinence education supporters use statistics such as these to demonstrate that their programs work better than comprehensive sex education.

Abstinence clubs and group movements that encourage people to take abstinence pledges

A Mom's Intuition

I got a permission slip for my oldest child in seventh grade to learn about puberty in science. . . . So, I went to go look at the curricula, and it [sic] was body parts, basically, then it was condoms and contraceptives. And I said to the teacher . . . "How do you get from body parts to condoms and contraceptives? There's a huge gap here." And he agreed, but he also said, "This is what the county gave me to teach." So I brought together a group of young people . . . and I asked them what they wanted to learn about with regard to sex. And it was amazing, the kind of answers they gave me. . . . "I want to learn about why guys"— the girls would say—"Why do guys say they're going to call and don't call?" And the guys would say, "Why do girls say don't touch me, don't touch me, but they wear these provocative clothes and this amazing perfume and lean up against me?. . . " "How do I know if I'm in love?" "How far is too far?" And I said, ". . . these are great questions. I'm going to find out the answer. . . ." So I went to several bookstores . . . and there really wasn't anything out there that was directed at kids. . . . People need this information.[3]

—Joneen Mackenzie, R.N., B.S.N., founder of WAIT Training

are becoming more common in the United States. People who support these movements argue that when something such as abstinence is made popular and talked about joyfully, it can become "cool." They believe more youth will want to practice abstinence if it is presented as a deliberate and positive choice. They worry that comprehensive sex education treats abstinence as something negative. They are also concerned that comprehensive sex educators claim that abstinence means a complete denial of something that can be pleasurable—sex. They hope to turn that perception around. ⌐

"Talking to your teen about sex can be a daunting task, but research shows they do listen to their parents. In fact, research also shows that parents' disapproval is the number-one reason teens abstain from sex before marriage. Our teens are listening; we must deliver the right message.

"What messages should parents give their teens? Certainly, accurate information about sexually transmitted diseases (STDs), unwed pregnancy, boundary setting, sexual intimacy and God's truth in Scripture are all vital subjects."[4]

—Linda Klepacki, R.N., M.P.H., Analyst for Sexual Health, Focus on the Family

Comedian Keith Deltano performs at an abstinence conference
in Hopkinsville, Kentucky.

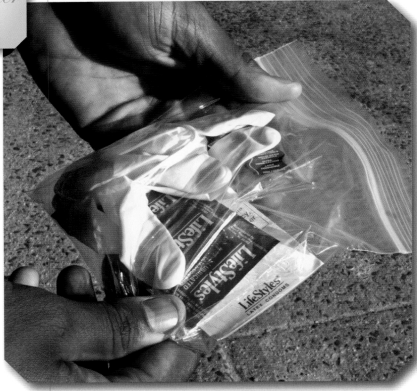

Some groups in favor of comprehensive sex education hand out contraceptives and literature about safer sex practices.

COMPREHENSIVE SEX EDUCATION

omprehensive sexual health educators and their supporters believe that young people need to be exposed to all options when it comes to making decisions related to sex. They also have research and statistics to back up their claims.

Provides Complete Information

Supporters of comprehensive sex education believe that complete and accurate sex-related information is vital for young people. They prefer to trust young people with the full scope of sex education topics and information that will help them make good decisions.

Supporters believe this education is necessary to inform youth of how to have safer sex if and when they engage in sexual activity. They argue that some of the skills taught in comprehensive sex education could be useful later in life. Even people who wait until marriage to have sex may need to know how to use birth control, recognize a sexually transmitted infection (STI), or advise a friend on one of those issues.

Supporters of comprehensive sex education also argue that fewer opportunities to learn facts about sex exist after students leave high school. Unless students take it upon themselves to seek a broad sexual education in college, they may never learn some important facts. They

WHO Study

The World Health Organization (WHO) conducted a study of 35 comprehensive sexual education programs around the world. The study found no evidence that comprehensive sexual education promotes sexual activity among youth. They found that comprehensive sexual education was more effective than abstinence education in promoting contraceptive use and safer sex practices.

Suzan Nolan is a retired school counselor. She says that comprehensive sex education would result in fewer unwanted pregnancies.

may also become susceptible to misinformation they receive later in life. Thus, comprehensive sex education supporters worry that public knowledge about sexual health topics will eventually be reduced.

PREPARES YOUTH FOR POSSIBILITY OF SEX

People who support comprehensive sex education believe it is inevitable that some young people will choose to have sex. They do not think that avoiding the subject of sex will prevent teenagers from experimenting with it. They contend that lack of information leaves young people vulnerable to making life-altering mistakes because they may not understand the full consequences of their actions.

"The governors are saying; 'Even if this administration is going to continue to push abstinence-only, we in the states are going to do the right thing by teens and actually give them the information they need to actually prevent an unintended pregnancy.'"[1]
—Cecile Richards, President, Planned Parenthood Federation of America

Supporters insist that if young people are going to have sex, comprehensive sex education will prepare them properly for it. They do not believe sex education encourages sexual activity among youth. Some believe it even discourages it, because the idea of pregnancy and STI transmission may provide a reality check for young couples interested in physical intimacy.

INCLUDES ABSTINENCE

Comprehensive sex educators are quick to remind their critics that comprehensive programs also discuss the value and benefits of abstinence. These programs describe abstinence as the only method of birth control that is 100 percent effective and the best way to prevent STI transmission. Comprehensive sex education supporters believe that abstinence is vital to their education program, and many of these educators are strong advocates of premarital abstinence for young people.

Supporters of comprehensive sex education claim that because their program includes recommending abstinence, it is inclusive and relevant to all students. Supporters believe that a comprehensive program can talk about the importance of emotional commitment in sexual relationships and why it is helpful to wait.

"Young people are going to learn about sex and our question has to be where do we want them to learn? From the media? From their friends? Or do we want them to learn from an educated, responsible adult?"[2]

—*Tamara Kreinin, President, Sexuality Information and Education Council of the United States*

CHALLENGING POP-CULTURE "WISDOM"

Comprehensive sex educators raise the point that youth will learn about sex whether or not the conversation is part of classroom learning. They believe it is better for youth to learn factual information from parents and teachers rather than getting pop-culture "wisdom" from their peers and the media. They are also concerned about misinformation that may lead youth to make irresponsible decisions while thinking that what they are doing is safe.

OPT-OUT POLICIES

In many school districts, parents who do not approve of the sex education programs have the option of removing their children from these programs. Some schools offer parents a chance to prescreen the information that will be presented in the sex education curriculum. Parents may come in to schools to view videos, pictures, and handouts. Sometimes teachers make each lesson plan available to parents. Some teachers are also available

Media Exposure

One goal of educators is to help students become independent thinkers. Teachers want their students to learn to listen to the facts, make well-informed decisions, and apply what they have learned to their lives. But teachers and parents are not always able to control exactly what ideas, images, and media their students and children are exposed to. According to writer Molly Masland,

In the debate over sex education, one thing is undisputed: The average kid today is immersed in sexual imagery. A generation that has grown up on the sordid details of the Starr Report, watched thong-clad teens gyrate on Spring Break cable specials, or read the cover of nearly any women's magazine in the grocery check-out line is familiar with the facts of life. But young people face a barrage of confusing messages. Along with titillating images from the media, some kids are told to "just say no" to sex. In school, others are taught how to put condoms on bananas in preparation for the real thing, and still other children receive no information whatsoever.[3]

Those in favor of comprehensive sex education want to help today's youth sort out the messages they receive so that they can make wise and informed decisions.

for questions about the curriculum and class assignments.

Supporters of comprehensive sex education believe opt-out policies bring the best choice to schools and parents. A comprehensive sex education program is available to those who want their children to participate in it. Those who object can take advantage of the opt-out policy.

Avoids Teaching Single Worldview

Comprehensive sex educators are concerned with ensuring that multiple views of sexuality are treated with respect in public school classrooms. They do not want to restrict all students' education to a worldview that may not be held by all students and their families. They believe that choice is an important part of every individual's sexual life, and people should not be made to feel bad about the sexual decisions they make.

Comprehensive sex educators believe that different choices may be appropriate for different people. In their view, the best way to prepare students to make sexual decisions is to present them with many options and allow them to choose their actions with confidence. ⌐

Some school districts allow parents to view sex education materials and discuss them with their child's teacher.

Comprehensive sex educators believe that understanding reproductive organs and sexual health is an important part of education.

TEACHING TOO LITTLE?

pponents of abstinence-only education strongly feel that excluding certain information from sex education is much more harmful to students than anything they could learn from a curriculum that explores all aspects of sexuality.

Naive View of Teen Sexuality

Opponents criticize abstinence educators for being too naive about teenage sexual activity. They argue that abstinence education fails to prepare youth for all possibilities. They see it as inevitable that some youth will choose to have sex before marriage, regardless of what they are taught. Even those opponents who agree that abstinence is best for teens may believe that some will not choose that path.

Leaves Youth at Risk of Unsafe Sex

Opponents say that youth who do have sex are more likely to engage in unsafe sex if they have only been taught abstinence. They use statistics to prove that it is irresponsible for educators not to teach youth about condom use and other safer sex practices. They argue that knowledge leads to safe choices, while ignorance leads to risky behavior.

In addition, some critics of abstinence education believe that abstinence-only programs teach misinformation in addition to leaving out important topics.

"Given the high stakes facing teens, the fact that almost half of all teens aged 15 to 19 years old in the United States have had sex, and the absence of research showing that 'abstinence-only' programs are effective, 'Just Say No' efforts are misleading at best, and dangerous at worst."[1]
— *NARAL Pro-Choice America Foundation*

Silence Breeds Shame and Secrecy

Opponents of abstinence education believe avoiding talk of sex makes people feel ashamed of their interest in sexuality. Throughout history, sex has often been a taboo subject in public conversation. Thus, it is often surrounded by secrecy, shame, guilt, and uncertainty. Opponents believe that abstinence education continues this negative association of sexuality. They believe open dialogue about sex topics will change this perception.

Government Accountability

The Government Accountability Office (GAO) is charged with monitoring government programs to ensure they are effective, safe, and beneficial to citizens. In 2006, the GAO released a study on the federal abstinence-only education funding program. In the report, the GAO commented on its concern that some abstinence education programs may include inaccurate information. The report stated:

These studies have reported that some of the materials used in abstinence-until-marriage education programs contain, for example, scientifically inaccurate information about anatomy and physiology as they relate to reproductive health as well as misleading information about contraceptive failure rates and STDs. . . . Further, studies examining the effectiveness of these programs have reported varied results. For example, some researchers have reported that abstinence-until-marriage education programs have resulted in adolescents reporting less frequent sexual intercourse or fewer sexual partners, while other researchers have reported that these types of programs did not affect the frequency of sexual intercourse or were ineffective in delaying the initiation of sexual intercourse.[2]

Opponents worry that maintaining a culture of shame around sexuality discourages youth from asking questions. They believe it is important for youth to have open dialogue with positive adult role models who help teens express their curiosity about sex in a healthy way.

Encourages Early Marriage

Some opponents of abstinence education believe that abstinence pledges may lead to early marriages, which they say lead more often to divorce. They believe that if young people feel shame about premarital sex, some of them may rush into marriage before they are ready so they can have sex. These opponents feel that emphasizing marriage, rather than any committed long-term relationship, places too much pressure on young couples. Additionally, opponents of abstinence education argue that even

Abstinence Program Reviews

The GAO study looked at ten states to study the effectiveness and accuracy of their abstinence education materials. In October 2006, GAO reported:

"Not all states that receive funding from ACF [Administration for Children and Families] have chosen to review their program materials for scientific accuracy. In particular, 5 of the 10 states that GAO contacted conduct such reviews. . . . While the extent to which federally funded abstinence-until-marriage education materials are inaccurate is not known, in the course of their reviews . . . some states reported that they have found inaccuracies in abstinence-until-marriage education materials. For example, one state official described an instance in which abstinence-until-marriage materials incorrectly suggested that HIV can pass through condoms because the latex used in condoms is porous."[3]

These protesters criticize the spread of abstinence-only education.

after marriage, some couples may want to use birth control for family planning.

Opponents also challenge the assumption that premarital sex is morally wrong. They suggest that some people may choose to follow a different moral code, and those people should not be forced to conform to a particular standard. They believe abstinence education takes a very narrow view of what is appropriate and that it can be hurtful to generalize about everyone's situation.

EXCLUDES HOMOSEXUAL YOUTH

In addition, opponents of abstinence education sometimes raise the point that the emphasis on marriage excludes homosexual youth. In most states, same-sex marriages are not currently allowed, so it is possible that youth who identify as gay and lesbian might not ever be able to get married. Does that mean those young people can never have sex in their lives? These opponents believe teaching such a lesson to students is unnecessarily harsh.

In addition, opponents worry that emphasizing marriage may lead homosexual youth to ignore all sex education if they feel it is not relevant to them. They worry that this will lead some students to participate in unsafe sex. They argue that a school education program should not teach beliefs that inherently exclude any student. They believe this is a form of discrimination. However, some states have begun to look differently at same-sex marriage, so it is possible that this argument may be less relevant in the future.

Advocates for Youth's View

According to Advocates for Youth, a nonprofit organization, the government's standards for abstinence education are skewed: It claims that "after a decade of extravagant funding, the government's own long-term research has clearly shown that abstinence-only programs do *not* delay sexual initiation *nor* do they reduce rates of either teen pregnancy or sexually transmitted infections (STIs)."[4]

No Chance to Opt In

Opponents of abstinence education do not like that a child's sex education may be limited by other people's views of sexuality. They argue that abstinence education offers no opt-in policy for parents who would like their children to learn more. They believe this is unfair to some students, who might benefit from comprehensive sex education.

For parents who know or suspect that their teenager is already sexually active, abstinence-only sex education does not offer discussions and information on safer sex for their children. These parents may believe abstinence would be better, but still want their children to engage in safer sex if they are having sex. Opponents of abstinence education worry that this sector of sexually active students is being overlooked and repeating lessons of abstinence may not be the most helpful.

"The attempts to maintain a uniform orthodox opinion among teachers should be opposed. The attempts of educational authorities to inject into public school and college instruction propaganda in the interest of any particular theory of society to the exclusion of others should be opposed."[5]
—from the American Civil Liberties Union creed, (#9.—Liberty in Education)

Actress Kate Walsh, center, is outspoken about her belief in the need for comprehensive and medically accurate sex education.

Protesters picket a sex education conference for teenagers sponsored by Planned Parenthood.

Too Much Information?

Opponents of comprehensive sex education also feel strongly about the issue. They worry about what information young people are being exposed to through these programs. They also criticize the way material is presented in a public, matter-of-fact way, as if sex behavior is expected of all teenagers.

Perhaps the major concern among opponents is that comprehensive sex education will entice youth to have sex. They believe that talking about sexual activity makes it more interesting to young people. They worry that sex education in school will encourage young people to become sexually active.

CONDONES PREMARITAL SEX

Opponents claim that teaching comprehensive sex education implies approval of premarital sex. They believe talking about topics such as birth control and sexual acts makes it seem more acceptable for young people.

Opponents of comprehensive sex education are against the message that sex is acceptable within any "committed" relationship. They disagree with the suggestion that youth should simply wait until they are "ready," "mature," or in a "committed monogamous

"We believe it's an inconsistent message. If you say, 'don't do it, it's not healthy for you, but if you're going to do it, do it this way,' that sends mixed signals to kids. [It only provides] a means for them to live an unhealthy lifestyle."[1]
—Lori Cole, Executive Director, Eagle Forum

relationship." They believe these terms are too abstract for teenagers to truly understand. They suggest that teenagers may have a skewed view of commitment and permanence. Marriage, they say, is a much more concrete idea, even to young people. Abstinence educators want the importance of marriage to be upheld.

MIXED MESSAGES

Opponents of comprehensive sex education are not appeased by promises to discuss abstinence as an important option. They believe that the principles of abstinence are weakened when immediately followed by instructions on how to have sex, if one chooses to.

Opponents of comprehensive sex education believe it is dangerous to spend time discussing behaviors that they contend should be discouraged. They believe that sending mixed messages confuses students.

Parent Views

According to a poll conducted for the National Abstinence Education Association: "Once they understand what abstinence education actually teaches, 6 out of 10 parents would rather their child receive abstinence education vs. comprehensive sex education. Only 3 out of 10 prefer comprehensive."[2]

A billboard in Baltimore, Maryland

This confusion may lead youth to make poor decisions because they do not understand the difference between appropriate behavior and risky behavior.

TREATS TEEN SEX AS INEVITABLE

Those who oppose comprehensive sex education also take issue with the claim that teen sex is inevitable. They feel strongly that teen sex is preventable, if youth are properly educated in abstinence. By talking about teenage sex as if it is expected, youth may feel pressured into sexual activity and think that all their peers are having sex. Some argue that peer pressure is enough of a problem without adding pressure from adults in classroom instruction.

Peer pressure is an issue that both sides of the debate recognize. Both sides are concerned about peer pressure urging youth into early sexual activity. Opponents of comprehensive sex education believe that classroom sex instruction may make youth feel the need to be sexually active, as they perceive their peers to be. Those who favor abstinence education believe it is a positive form of peer pressure that needs to be represented more.

Makes Sex Talk Too Casual

Opponents of comprehensive sex education often have concerns that these programs treat sex too casually. Using frank language and encouraging open dialogue are hallmarks of comprehensive sex education. However, some opponents feel that sex should be treated with more respect and spoken of discreetly only in very specific, deliberate circumstances. Opponents also are concerned that frank talk about sex interferes with young people's modesty and innocence.

PROMOTES FALSE MORALITY

Those who oppose comprehensive sex education often return to the argument that premarital sex is morally wrong. Some believe this alone is sufficient reason not to talk about sex in schools. The vast majority of students are not married or engaged. Opponents of comprehensive

"Popular" Sex Education

Sex and romantic relationships have always been discussed in popular culture. Magazines, books, television shows, and films deal with sex. Much of what most people learn about human sexuality comes from the media. How sex is handled in the media and popular culture has changed over time.

Mainstream television shows used to show twin beds in married couples' bedrooms. This was to avoid filming them sleeping in the same bed. Today, it is not uncommon to see television couples in bed together, naked, as if they have just had sex. Full nudity is not shown, but is suggested.

Fashion and advertising also make their mark on sexuality. The steady rise of dress hemlines between 1900 and 2000 indicates how the public has become more comfortable with the human body and sexuality. At one time, it was scandalous for a woman to show her ankles in public. Later, anything above the knees was considered too short. Then, mini-skirts became popular. Walking on beaches in the United States today, people can view almost total public nudity with people wearing string bikinis and the briefest of swim trunks.

Abstinence educators take a negative view of most modern media images of sexuality. They believe these images contribute to peer pressure for young people to experiment with sex.

sex education contend it is morally inappropriate for youth to be exposed to such topics.

Some opponents point out that comprehensive sex education is not open to a range of moral views. It promotes a single, very problematic moral code. They claim that moral code discusses the possibility that sex before marriage is appropriate for some people. Opponents do not agree that this message should be given or even implied to youth.

Some also believe comprehensive sex education undermines religious traditions. For instance, some faith groups believe birth control is morally wrong even in marriage, so it is sinful and wrong for youth to learn about it. Traditionally, the Roman Catholic Church has opposed the use of artificial birth control methods. In 1968, Pope Paul VI publicly reaffirmed the Roman Catholic Church's belief that using birth control is immoral, even in marriage.

States Not Taking a Stand

As of 2008, no state requires abstinence-only education, though some states emphasize it. Fourteen states require both abstinence and contraception be taught. Nineteen states specifically require abstinence, but allow contraception to be taught. Seventeen states do not regulate their local school boards' decisions about sex education.

These girls sign a banner promoting abstinence at a music festival in Minnesota.

Dr. Mary Steichen Calderone was president of the Sexuality Information and Education Council of the United States (SIECUS) until 1982.

Players in the Debate

Many groups and organizations are involved in the sex education debate. Some organizations exist for the sole purpose of advancing either abstinence education or comprehensive sex education. Other organizations involved in the debate exist for very different purposes, but support one view or the other.

In Favor of Abstinence-only

The National Abstinence Clearinghouse (NAC) is the nation's largest network of abstinence educators. Based in South Dakota, the NAC's mission is to

> *promote the appreciation for and practice of sexual abstinence (purity) until marriage through the distribution of age appropriate, factual and medically-referenced materials. We are a clearinghouse for abstinence in-formation and a network of abstinence advocates.* [1]

NAC's Advisory Council consists of nationally known abstinence educators. NAC also has the Medical Abstinence Council, which is made up of physicians who will not promote or prescribe contraceptives to unmarried teenagers.

NAC regularly hosts conferences on abstinence education. It provides materials, training, and resources for abstinence educators and their supporters. NAC's work occurs at the national, regional, and local levels, in addition to some international efforts.

The National Abstinence Education Association (NAEA) was founded in 2006. The organization was created by a group of leaders who support abstinence education.

NAEA lobbies elected officials to support policies that promote abstinence education. The NAEA works to help abstinence be viewed in a positive light in the media and in public perception. It conducts research on abstinence and sexuality and provides training and resources for abstinence educators.

The WAIT (Why Am I

Defining "Risk"

People on both sides of the sex education debate view the concept of "risk" very differently.

To an abstinence educator, there is no such thing as "safer sex." Abstinence is the only way to be safe. As every sex act has inherent risk, it is false to teach about safety and protection in sexual activity. They do not agree that risk is reduced by "safer sex" practices. They argue that the risks in premarital sex are emotional as well as physical. They believe it always harms people to have premarital sex. To those who support abstinence, the sex act has negative consequences that will occur whether or not it results in a sexually transmitted infection (STI) or an unexpected pregnancy.

To a comprehensive sex educator, whatever is done to minimize the chances of STI transmission is considered protective, safer behavior. They agree that there is always some risk in sexual activity, but they believe that people should learn how to minimize the risk. They do not agree that premarital sex is always emotionally damaging. They teach people to delay having sex until they are committed and ready in order to avoid emotional scars. But, they say even emotionally healthy sex can have physical consequences that people must learn how to protect themselves against.

Tempted?) Training program began in 1992. Trained as a nurse, Joneen Mackenzie was alarmed by the way reproduction and sex education information was handled in her son's middle school science class. She thought two key components of sex education were missing: the building of a relationship and practicing abstinence. She gathered a group of teenagers and asked them what they wanted to learn about sex. WAIT Training emerged as a response to their questions.

WAIT Training began by developing materials about abstinence, healthy relationships, and marriage for schools and nonprofit organizations. In 2003, it became incorporated as an educational nonprofit organization. WAIT Training strives to strengthen marriage, promote abstinence, and help youth build the life skills to form lasting, healthy relationships.

Causation

People on both sides of the debate think very differently about what causes people to act in certain ways.

For example, abstinence educators believe talking about specific sexual behavior will lead people to do those things. They believe talking about virginity and abstinence instead will lead more people to wait.

Comprehensive sex educators believe people will have sex whether or not it is talked about. By talking about it, people can learn how to be safer in their sexual behavior. They believe not talking about specific sexual behavior will lead people to do those things without using protection.

In Favor of Comprehensive Sex Education

The Sexuality Information and Education Council of the United States (SIECUS) mission statement reads:

> *SIECUS affirms that sexuality is a fundamental part of being human, one that is worthy of dignity and respect. We advocate for the right of all people to accurate information, comprehensive education about sexuality, and sexual health services. SIECUS works to create a world that ensures social justice and sexual rights.* [2]

Professionals who saw a need for better-organized efforts for comprehensive sex education established SIECUS in 1964. The organization helps people access information about all aspects of human sexuality. SIECUS provides resources for professionals and individuals, trains sexual health educators, and advocates for public policies that promote positive views of human sexuality. This includes comprehensive sex education in

Opposite Statistics

A report by NARAL Pro-Choice America shows that seven in ten Americans oppose using federal funds for abstinence-only programs that exclude information on contraception. The poll was conducted by Hickman-Brown Research, Inc.

A report by The National Abstinence Education Association shows that six out of ten parents think more government funding should be given to abstinence education instead of comprehensive sex education. They report that only two out of ten parents want more funding for comprehensive sex education.

Missouri Senator Delbert Scott sponsored a bill that would allow schools to offer abstinence-only courses.

schools. SIECUS also works to keep media outlets updated on their policy interests.

Brought together by SIECUS, the National Coalition to Support Sexuality Education (NCSSE) is a network of more than 140 organizations. They advocate that all children and youth in the United States should be exposed to accurate, age-appropriate, comprehensive sex education. NCSSE serves as a central meeting location for these organizations, many of which have very different missions from one another. NCSSE member groups include health care professionals, educators, religious groups, child advocates, and public policy groups.

Founded in 1916, the Planned Parenthood Federation of America strives

> *to be the nation's most trusted provider of sexual and reproductive health care; an authoritative and passionate advocate for our clients and society; and at the forefront of developing the next generation of leaders of the sexual and reproductive health and social justice movement.*[3]

"Sexual health is a state of physical, emotional, mental and social well being in relation to sexuality; it is not merely the absence of disease, dysfunction or infirmity. Sexual health requires a positive and respectful approach to sexuality and sexual relationships, as well as the possibility of having pleasurable and safe sexual experiences, free of coercion, discrimination and violence."[4]

—*World Health Organization, 2002*

Planned Parenthood affiliates provide health-care information and support to women and men. It manages more than 860 health clinics nationwide. Education programs are offered on women's health issues, sex education, family planning, and healthy relationships.

The Planned Parenthood Action Fund is a related organization that works to promote comprehensive sex education through advocacy, voter education, and lobbying elected officials. ⌐

Planned Parenthood headquarters in Boston, Massachusetts

Some states give strict guidelines regarding what can be taught about sex.

THE CHALLENGE
FOR SCHOOLS

People on both sides of the sex education debate agree that youth need positive influences in order to make good choices. Still, with so many different opinions about sex education, it can be difficult for schools to decide how to structure their sex education classes. Schools must determine how much information is appropriate. How much is too much? Is it possible to teach too little? It is a challenge to find a balance between pleasing parents, protecting students, providing positive influence, and presenting accurate information on all sexual health topics.

PARENT PERSPECTIVES

Some parents have strong religious views. Some have concerns about the rate of teen sexual activity. Some feel discomfort in talking about sex topics with teenagers. These issues all drive the debate in different ways.

Parents overwhelmingly hope that their children will choose abstinence. According to a survey by the National Abstinence Education Association, nine out of ten parents agree that sexual abstinence is the best choice for their children's health and future. However, not all parents believe abstinence training is the only sexual education that teenagers need. A survey by National Public Radio, the Kaiser Medical Group, and others revealed that 99 percent of Americans believe it is appropriate to teach youth about sexually transmitted infections (STIs), and

94 percent believe it is appropriate to teach youth about birth control. Statistics, however, do not solve the problem. Though most people appear to agree that abstinence is best, that does not answer the question of how to deal with other information.

NATIONAL YOUTH RISK BEHAVIOR SURVEY

Both sides are interested in determining how many teenagers engage in sexual activity and how often. The national Youth Risk Behavior Survey (YRBS) is

State Mandates

According to the National Coalition to Support Sexuality Education, the following are examples of state regulations for sex education:

California does not require schools to provide sex education, but has guidelines for schools that choose to offer it. Schools must respect diversity, be medically accurate, and include lessons on contraception. Schools must notify parents and offer an opt-out policy.

Indiana requires schools to provide sex education emphasizing abstinence until marriage and monogamy within marriage. State law does not limit other components of instruction. Parents must be offered an opt-out policy.

Louisiana does not require schools to provide HIV or STI education and prevention information. Schools are allowed to provide sex education for students in grade six, but are not allowed to provide any for younger students. All grades are prohibited from learning positive messages about homosexuality and abortion.

New York requires all students to participate in health education from kindergarten through grade six. In grades 7 through 12, separate half-year classes of health education are required. Students must be taught about HIV/AIDS and how to prevent its transmission. Abstinence is emphasized as the best form of STI transmission prevention. Schools offer parents an opt-out policy.

an ongoing study conducted by the Centers for Disease Control (CDC). Based in Atlanta, Georgia, the CDC monitors a wide range of illnesses, infectious diseases, and other health risks on a national and international basis.

The YRBS "monitors priority health risk behaviors that contribute to the leading causes of death, disability, and social problems among youth and adults in the United States."[1] The national YRBS is conducted every two years during the spring semester and collects data representative of public and private school students in grades 9 through 12 throughout the United States.

The 2005 survey found that:

❖ 46.8 percent of teens had ever had sexual intercourse.

❖ 33.3 percent of teens were currently sexually active at the time of the survey.

A More Even Split?

According to a 2004 poll by National Public Radio, the Kaiser Family Foundation, and Harvard University's Kennedy School of Government, U.S. citizens are closely divided about the best general approach to teaching sex and sexuality in schools. The poll asked people to choose which of these two statements they most agreed with:
(1) When it comes to sex, teenagers need to have limits set; they must be told what is acceptable and what is not.
(2) Ultimately teenagers need to make their own decisions, so their education needs to be more in the form of providing information and guidance.

Responses were nearly tied: 47 percent selected the first statement and 51 percent selected the second. More parents of seventh and eighth graders chose the first statement (53 percent) than the second (45 percent). Parents of high school students were evenly divided.

sex educati

sex ed • u • ca • tion

Jonathan Stacks is the campaign manager for the Illinois Campaign for Responsible Sex Education, and supports comprehensive sex education.

❖ 62.8 percent of sexually active teens had used condoms during their last sexual intercourse.

❖ 87.9 percent had been taught in school about HIV/AIDS infection.

People on both sides of the debate find these statistics discouraging. Abstinence educators believe the rate of teen sex is too high. They see it as a sign that more talk of abstinence is needed. Comprehensive sex educators consider the rate of condom use too low. They see it as a sign that more education on contraception and preventing the transmission of STIs is needed.

Student Perspectives

Students also find ways to voice their thoughts. On one side, abstinence pledge groups promote purity pledges and speak of the value of sex-free teen years. Abstinence clubs are popular in some high schools, and there is also a growing abstinence movement on college campuses across the country. Abstinence clubs may hold regular meetings or events designed to be positive, friendly, and free of sex-related peer pressure.

On the other side, networks of teen health educators emphasize comprehensive sex education through peer-to-peer sharing. Peer educators are usually trained by adult health professionals and given supervised opportunities to teach within their

College Sex Education Curricula

Many colleges and universities require incoming freshmen to participate in a short health education course before beginning their first semester. Topics covered in the course may include information on student health center resources, campus safety, campus emergency procedures, instructions for where to go when feeling ill, alcohol and drug information, and sexual health education. The sexual health component may cover how to obtain and use contraceptives, STI prevention information, and discussion of sexual violence and abuse.

"The kinds of skills young people develop as part of sex education are linked to more general life-skills. For example, being able to communicate, listen, negotiate, [and] ask for and identify sources of help and advice, are useful life-skills and can be applied in terms of sexual relationships."[2]
—*AVERT, AVERTing HIV and AIDS*

peer group. Some youth believe that removing adults from sexual health conversations makes teens more comfortable to ask questions and explore issues openly. Peer education programs are especially common on college campuses.

The Debate Continues

In 2008, Congress considered proposed legislation called the Responsible Education About Life (REAL) Act. This act would create federal funding for comprehensive sex education in addition to the existing funds that support abstinence-only sex education.

It appears that American society is not near a conclusion about what is better: comprehensive sex education or abstinence-only sex education. Either way, sex education is meant to give students the best set of information possible as they face the decision of whether or not to engage in sex. If youth choose a more responsible course of action because of what they learned in school, sex educators on both sides feel their work was worthwhile.

Whether or not they teach about sex, many teachers choose
to emphasize the importance of healthy relationships.

TIMELINE

1873

The Comstock Act prohibits distribution of immoral material, including birth control information, on March 3.

1904

Psychologist G. Stanley Hall first coins the term *adolescents.*

1916

Margaret Sanger establishes the first birth control clinic in the United States.

1941

The United States enters World War II. Women take jobs that were never open to them before, including in factories and offices.

1913

American Social Hygiene Association founders meet to discuss their goals for the organization.

1915

American Social Hygiene Association officially launches on February 14.

1945

World War II ends and many women return home to start families and become full-time mothers.

1960

U.S. Food and Drug Administration approves the sale of oral contraceptive pills on May 9.

TIMELINE

1964

Sexuality Information and Education Council of the United States is founded.

1965

On June 7, the U.S. Supreme Court rules in *Griswold v. Connecticut* that laws prohibiting birth control are unconstitutional.

1968

Pope Paul VI publicly reaffirms the Roman Catholic Church's belief that using artificial birth control is immoral, even in marriage, on June 29.

1999

Congress allocates funds for abstinence-only education.

2001

Funds are made available for communities that teach abstinence-only education.

1973

U.S. Supreme Court's *Roe v. Wade* decision legalizes abortion on January 22.

1981

The first reported appearances of acquired immunodeficiency syndrome (AIDS) are seen.

1996

President Bill Clinton signs an act that establishes new federal grants for abstinence-only education on August 22.

2006

The National Abstinence Education Association is founded.

2008

Congress considers the Responsible Education About Life (REAL) Act that would create federal funding for comprehensive sex education.

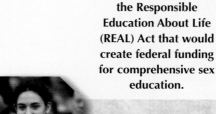

Essential Facts

At Issue

Abstinence-only Educators

❖ All communities, schools, and families should teach young people that abstinence before marriage is the best way to approach sexual behavior.

❖ Waiting to have sex is a good moral decision.

❖ If society talks more about abstinence, more people will choose to practice it.

❖ Teaching unmarried teens about safer sex sends mixed messages about when it is appropriate to have sex.

Comprehensive Sex Educators

❖ Young people should be educated about birth control and safer sex so that when and if they have sex, they will know how to protect themselves.

❖ It is unrealistic to believe that every person will choose to practice abstinence until marriage.

❖ Abstinence is a good choice for many people, but each person makes his or her sexual decisions based upon a number of different factors.

❖ Statistics show that some teens are having sex, so they need to know how to minimize the risks involved.

Critical Dates

1916

Margaret Sanger established the first birth control clinic in the United States. She later founded the American Birth Control League, which eventually became the Planned Parenthood Federation of America.

1960s

The U.S. Food and Drug Administration approved the sale of oral contraceptive pills. The U.S. Supreme Court ruled that laws prohibiting birth control are unconstitutional.

1980s

The first cases of AIDS are reported. Anxiety and uncertainty spread as the disease was researched.

2000s

Funds are made available for communities that teach abstinence-only sex education. Congress considers legislation that would create federal funding to teach comprehensive sex education.

Quotes

"Real abstinence education is essential to reducing out-of-wedlock childbearing, preventing sexually transmitted diseases, and improving emotional and physical well-being among the nation's youth. True abstinence education programs help young people to develop an understanding of commitment, fidelity, and intimacy that will serve them well as the foundations of healthy marital life in the future."—*Robert Rector, Senior Research Fellow, The Heritage Foundation*

"Young people are going to learn about sex and our question has to be where do we want them to learn? From the media? From their friends? Or do we want them to learn from an educated, responsible adult?"—*Tamara Kreinin, President, Sexuality Information and Education Council of the United States*

ADDITIONAL RESOURCES

SELECT BIBLIOGRAPHY

Agel, Jerome B. *We, the People: Great Documents of the American Nation*. New York: Barnes & Noble, 1997.

Bailey, Jacqui. *Sex, Puberty and All That Stuff: A Guide to Growing Up*. Hauppauge, NY: Barron's, 2004.

Howell, Marcela, and Marilyn Keefe. "The History of Federal Abstinence-Only Funding." *Advocates for Youth*. July 2007. 31 July 2008 <http://www.advocatesforyouth.org/publications/factsheet/fshistoryabonly.htm>.

Miller, James, and John Thompson. *The Almanac of American History*. Washington DC: National Geographic, 2006.

FURTHER READING

Cook, Bruce. *Parents, Teens, and Sex: The Big Talk Book*. Atlanta, GA: Choosing the Best Publishing, 2003.

Gowan, L. Kris. *Sexual Decisions: The Ultimate Teen Guide*. Lanham, MD: Rowman & Littlefield, 2007.

Luker, Kristin. *When Sex Goes to School*. New York: W.W. Norton & Co., 2006.

Web Links

To learn more about sex education in schools, visit ABDO Publishing Company online at **www.abdopublishing.com**. Web sites about sex education in schools are featured on our Book Links page. These links are routinely monitored and updated to provide the most current information available.

For More Information

For more information on this subject, contact or visit the following organizations.

Global Health Odyssey Museum (in association with the Smithsonian Institution)
Centers for Disease Control and Prevention
1600 Clifton Road, N.E. at CDC Parkway, Atlanta, GA 30333
404-639-0830
www.cdc.gov/gcc/exhibit
The Centers for Disease Control provides guided tours of its exhibitions to showcase its history and current work. The exhibits also provide information on infectious and chronic diseases, health risks, illness prevention, and healthy lifestyles.

Robert Crown Center for Health Education (affiliated with The Museum of Science and Industry)
57th Street and Lake Shore Drive, Chicago, IL 60637
773-684-1414
www.robertcrown.org
The Crown Center offers programs for youth of all ages on health topics. In partnership with Chicago's Museum of Science and Industry, it offers a class discussing puberty, human reproduction, fetus development, and childbirth.

Glossary

abstinence
   Refraining from sexual activity.

adolescents
   Young people between puberty and maturity.

AIDS
   Acquired immunodeficiency syndrome, an illness that weakens the human immune system, making an affected person vulnerable to rare and serious illnesses.

birth control
   Devices that make sex less likely to result in pregnancy.

chastity
   Abstaining from sexual intercourse.

component
   An important part of the whole.

comprehensive
   Covering completely and including all topics.

contraceptives
   Birth control items to prevent or lessen the possibility of pregnancy.

dialogue
   A conversation or discussion.

grant
   A donation of money to a project or organization to continue their work.

HIV
   Human immunodeficiency virus, the virus that causes AIDS.

homosexual
   Being sexually attracted to people of the same sex.

hygiene
   Cleanliness and self-care.

intimacy
   Physical or emotional closeness with someone else.

legislation

Laws enacted by the government.

mandate

An order or requirement.

monogamy

Being in a sexual relationship with one person only.

moral

Something that is right or appropriate, based on values.

pandemic

A disease that has spread to many geographical locations.

policy

A law, rule, or guideline.

reproduction

The biological process of conception, pregnancy, and childbirth.

safer sex

Use of birth control to prevent pregnancy and/or barriers to prevent sexually transmitted infections.

school board

A group of local officials responsible for managing decisions for a school district.

sexual health

The state of mental, emotional, and physical well-being in relation to sex.

sexual revolution

A social movement that changes public standards or perceptions of sexuality.

sexuality

Thoughts, feelings, beliefs, and actions related to attraction and sex.

STI

Sexually transmitted infection.

SOURCE NOTES

Chapter 1. Safer Sex versus Abstinence
1. Jerry Gramckow. "The Real Values Behind 'Values-Free' Sex Education." *Focus on the Family*. 1 July 2008 <http://www.family.org/socialissues/A000001082.cfm>.

Chapter 2. Sex Education in U.S. History
1. Maggie Gallagher. "The Stakes: Why We Need Marriage." *National Review Online*. 14 July 2003. 1 July 2008 <http://www.nationalreview.com/comment/comment-gallagher071403.asp>.

Chapter 3. Sex Education Topics
None.

Chapter 4. Government Responsibility
1. "About the First Amendment." *First Amendment Center*. 30 June 2008 <http://www.firstamendmentcenter.org/about.aspx?item=about_firstamd>.
2. "'Abstinence-only' Programs: Ideology over Science." *NARAL Pro-Choice America Foundation*. 3 Mar. 2008. 1 July 2008 <http://www.prochoiceamerica.org/assets/files/Sex-Ed-Ab-Only-Ideology.pdf>. 3; GAO-08-66-4T>. 7.

Chapter 5. Abstinence-only Education

1. "'Abstinence-only' Programs: Ideology over Science." *NARAL Pro-Choice America Foundation*. 3 Mar. 2008. 1 July 2008 <http://www.prochoiceamerica.org/assets/files/Sex-Ed-Ab-Only-Ideology.pdf>. 4.

2. Robert Rector. "The Effectiveness of Abstinence Education Programs in Reducing Sexual Activity." *The Heritage Foundation*. 8 Apr. 2002. 1 July 2008 <http://www.heritage.org/Research/Abstinence/BG1533.cfm>.

3. Joneen Mackenzie. Video. "About Us: The Origins of WAIT Training." 1 July 2008 <http://www.waittraining.org/about_origins_healthy_marriage_relationships_sexual_abstinence_education.asp>.

4. Linda Klepacki. "Dear Parents: What Your Teens Need to Know About Sex." *Focus on the Family*. 1 July 2008 <http://www.family.org/socialissues/A000001081.cfm>.

Chapter 6. Comprehensive Sex Education

1. Sheryl Attkisson. "States Rejecting 'Abstinence-Only' Funding." *CBS News.com*. 7 Jan. 2008. 1 July 2008 <http://www.cbsnews.com/stories/2008/01/07/eveningnews/main3680520.shtml>.

2. Molly Masland. "Carnal Knowledge: The sex ed debate." *MSNBC.com*. 1 July 2008 <http://www.msnbc.msn.com/id/3071001/>.

3. Ibid.

Source Notes Continued

Chapter 7. Teaching Too Little?

1. "'Abstinence-only' Programs: Ideology over Science." *NARAL Pro-Choice America Foundation*. 3 Mar. 2008. 1 July 2008 <http://www.prochoiceamerica.org/assets/files/Sex-Ed-Ab-Only-Ideology.pdf>. 7.

2. "Abstinence Education: Efforts to Assess the Accuracy and Effectiveness of Federally Funded Programs." *Government Accountability Office*. Oct 2006. 1 July 2008 <http://www.gao.gov/new.items/d0787.pdf>. 2.

3. Ibid. 16.

4. Marcela Howell and Marilyn Keefe. "The History of Federal Abstinence-Only Funding." *Advocates for Youth*. July 2007. 1 July 2008 <http://www.advocatesforyouth.org/publications/factsheet/fshistoryabonly.htm>.

5. Jerome B. Agel. *We, the People: Great Documents of the American Nation.* New York: Barnes & Noble, 1997. 132.

Chapter 8. Too Much Information?

1. Molly Masland. "Carnal Knowledge: The sex ed debate." *MSNBC.com*. 1 July 2008 <http://www.msnbc.msn.com/id/3071001/>.

2. "Zogby International Poll: Parental Support for Abstinence Education." *National Abstinence Education Association*. 3 May 2007. 1 July 2008 <http://www.abstinenceassociation.org/newsroom/050307_zogby_key_findings.html>.

3. Doug Kirby. *Family Planning Perspectives*. Nov/Dec 1991. WAIT Training. 5 Nov. 2008 <http://www.why-abstinence.org/abstinence_education_facts_figures.asp>.

Chapter 9. Players in the Debate

1. *National Abstinence Clearinghouse*. 1 July 2008 <http://www.abstinence.net/about/>.
2. "About Us." *SIECUS*. 1 July 2008 <http://www.siecus.org/index.cfm?fuseaction=Page.viewPage&pageId=472>.
3. "Vision for the Planned Parenthood National Plan of Action for 2008–2011." Annual Report 2006–2007. *Planned Parenthood*. 1 July 2008 <http://www.plannedparenthood.org/files/AR_2007_vFinal.pdf>. 2.
4. "Sexual Health." World Health Organization working definition. *Centers for Disease Control*. 1 July 2008 <http://www.cdc.gov/sexualhealth/>.

Chapter 10. The Challenge for Schools

1. "National Youth Risk Behavior Survey 1991–2005: Trends in the Prevalence of Sexual Behavior." *Centers for Disease Control*. 1 July 2008 <http://www.cdc.gov/HealthyYouth/YRBS/pdf/trends/2005_YRBS_Sexual_Behaviors.pdf>.
2. "Sex education that works." *AVERT.org*. 18 Aug 2008 <http://www.avert.org/sexedu.htm>.

INDEX

ABOUT THE AUTHOR

Kekla Magoon is the author of several fiction and nonfiction books for young adults. She especially enjoys writing about history and social studies.

PHOTO CREDITS

Cheryl Senter/AP Images, cover; Kevin P. Casey/AP Images, 6, 11, 95; Anthony S. Bush/AP Images, 15; John Lent/AP Images, 16; Robert W. Klein/AP Images, 22; Sherwin Crasto/AP Images, 27; Andy Sawyer/AP Images, 28; Kira Horvath/Star Ledger/Corbis, 32; Danny Vowell/AP Images, 37, 55; Chitose Suzuki/AP Images, 38, 47; Massimo Sambucetti/AP Images, 43; Preston McConkie/AP Images, 48; Daniel Miller/AP Images, 51; Robert Mecea/AP Images, 56; Joe Kafka/AP Images, 58; AP Images, 63; Corbis, 64; Jeff Fusco/Getty Images, 68; Joshua Roberts/Getty Images, 71; Duane A. Laverty/AP Images, 72; Gail Burton/AP Images, 75; Bill Zimmer/AP Images, 79; J. Harris/AP Images, 80; Kelley McCall/AP Images, 85; Charles Krupa/AP Images, 87; Desiree Hunter/AP Images, 88; Seth Perlman/AP Images, 92